MW01503985

i am life

Andy Branham

Published by Andy Branham
Printed in the United States of America
ISBN: 9798312567571

For more of my work, visit: @theandybranham on all social media.

i am life–2

To Momma,

for all of the trouble I've caused.

Foreword

Thank you for picking up my second book!

Life is a story we write every day. Some pages are filled with joy, some with pain, some with laughter, and some with lessons we never saw coming. *i am life* is the story of mine—told in moments, in memories, in poetry. It's not a grand epic or a tragedy, just a life lived as honestly as I could manage.

Even though this book follows my life in order, I feel that it can be consumed in any way the reader wishes. *i am life* reminds me of one of the best gifts I've ever received. On my 18th birthday, after all the main presents had been opened, my dad casually walked into my room and dropped a binder on my bed. Inside were letters he had written to me over the first 18 years of my life. It's the most thoughtful and impressive present I'll ever receive (sorry). The last letter, in particular, stuck with me. It was filled with some of the best advice I've ever read. I go back to it often, rereading the words he left me, and in many ways, that letter inspired the way I chose to end this collection.

I never expected poetry to be where I'd end up. I only have one book under my belt, but it took so much time and energy that I felt drained by the end. It's not that I stopped loving storytelling—I just needed something different. Something fresh. Something that didn't require planning out every twist and turn, every conversation, every arc. I wanted to write in a way that felt free, that let me spill everything onto the page without worrying if it all made perfect sense. And that's how I landed on poetry.

I love keeping people on their toes. You read a long, fictional story and think, *Where's he gonna go from here?* Boom—poetry. How about that? At first, it was just an experiment, but the more I wrote, the more I realized this was exactly what I needed. Poetry let me take the tangled mess of thoughts in my head and turn them into something real. It didn't need to follow rules, didn't need to fit into a box—it just had to be honest.

This book isn't just a collection of poems. It's my life. The highs, the lows, the moments of clarity, the mistakes I've made, the lessons I've learned. I started this journey with little experience in poetry, but I quickly realized something: poetry isn't about perfection. It's about expression. These poems are real. They are who I was, who I am, and who I hope to become.

Hopefully, you find something in these pages that speaks to you. If you just enjoy the ride, that's great too. Either way, thank you for being here.

—Andy Branham

i am life

Hallmark

Light from dark, I will rise anew,
A birthmark formed, a sign of you.
Love surrounds, a sky so blue,
No doubt, no pause, just warmth from you.

You welcome me with open arms,
No question marks, no raised alarms.
A hallmark etched, both old and new,
I am of you, and you of me too.

Small Arms, Big Heart

Three years ahead, yet still so small,
Tiny hands, but they held it all.
Soft and warm, your touch so light,
A brother's love, pure and bright.

No lessons taught, yet you just knew,
How to hold, how to soothe.
Wide-eyed wonder, your fingers curled,
You cradled me against the world.

No burden, no doubt, no fear inside,
Felt joy, felt pride, a warmth inside.
A child's heart, yet strong and free,
Before I knew love, you loved me.

Mountain & Goddess

My Daddy stood, a mountain tall,
Unshaken, steady—above it all.
A hero cloaked in warmth and might,
Chewbacca's twin, in my young sight.

His laughter rumbled, deep and bold,
Arms like stone, yet soft to hold.
He carried worlds upon his back,
Yet never let his love grow slack.

And then my Momma—golden, bright,
A goddess bathed in morning light.
Her touch, the only home I knew,
A heart so full, so kind, so true.

She took me where the wild winds played,
Her mirror image, hand-in-hand we stayed.
Her love was trips, was whispered songs,
Was knowing I was where I belonged.

Two pillars, standing firm and wide,
The safest place, where love resides.

The Cassatt Tree Monster

Out past the roads where dust runs free,
Sat a home wrapped in old oak trees.
A trailer lived in, worn just right,
A beacon glowing soft at night.

Papa, a mountain, hands of steel,
Could build, could mend, could make things real.
With knowing eyes, a steady stance,
He spun us stories—wild, entranced.

Beware the Cassatt Tree Monster's call,
Lurking where the cypress tree falls.
We'd huddle close, but laugh inside,
Safe with the man who never lies.

And oh, the pool, the endless days,
Splashing loud in summer's haze.
My brother, cousin, side by side,
In Nana's care, hearts open wide.

Nana, small but love so vast,
A warmth that outshone every past.
Her heart could fill the widest sea,
A love worth forty men, you see.

Her arms, a haven, soft but strong,
The place I'd go when things went wrong.
Her voice, a melody so pure.

Weekends spent where love ran deep,
In Cassatt's arms, our dreams would keep.

The Beagle's Bark

Out in Lugoff, a house so small,
But filled with love, with joy, with all.
Grandpa's chair, his throne, his seat,
A pillar of strength, steady and neat.
A quiet power, a loyal friend.
Through every storm, through every test,
He stood so firm, he gave his best.
With wisdom etched in every line,
His presence was a force divine.

Grandma with her wit and grace,
A twinkle in her eye, a smile on her face.
She'd laugh at the beagle's constant bark,
While making a snide comment in the dark.
Her love was felt in every space,
In every room, in every place.
Her hands were soft, yet sharp with care,
Her heart a warmth beyond compare.

And oh, the board games we would play,
Laughter filling every day.
The beagle's bark, a constant sound,

Chasing us 'round and 'round and 'round.
In that little house, we found our way,
In their love, we'd always stay.
No space for sorrow, no room for fear,
Only joy and warmth, forever near.

Bunny Ears

All morning long, I twisted and tried,
Bunny ears, through the loop, I cried!
Finally, I did it—oh what a feat!
My right shoe tied up, so neat, so sweet.

I ran to Momma, my joy so wide,
Look, I did it! I beamed with absolute pride.
Then I took off the shoe and set it aside,
On the stand by the door, where it would reside.

When Daddy came home, I ran to him fast,
To show him my shoe, a moment to last.

Friendship Kicks Off

The world was big, my heart unsure,
A shy step forward, a friendship's door.
Faces unknown, but smiles were kind,
And slowly, I began to find—

In every game, in every play,
A place to be, a world to stay.
The ball at my feet, the field alive,
I learned to breathe, to run, to strive.

With friends beside, the world felt wide,
On green turf, I could slide and slide.
The game, the rush, the victory call,
In soccer, I stood so proud and tall.

The teammates, the laughter, the cheers so loud,
I found my rhythm, my place in the crowd.
A sport, a love, a bond with a crew,
I kicked my way into something new.

Schoolyard

The halls felt long, the days so slow,
Books and desks, where did they go?
Not yet my world, not yet my place,
But friends I found, a smiling face.

We laughed, we ran, we passed the time,
A break from books, a climb to climb.
The schoolyard game, the shared delight,
Made every day feel somehow bright.

Spelling it out

Feel the breeze, so wild, so free,

Running fast where I'm meant to be.

Every road, a path untold,

Every dream, a hand to hold.

Doubts may chase, but I won't hide,

Open skies, my heart's my guide.

My own two feet will choose the ride.

SpongeBob

Underwater laughter, a yellow friend,
The episodes played, the jokes would blend.
SpongeBob, Patrick, and the crew,
Their silly antics, always new.

Laughter echoed, the world was bright,
Cartoons that made my heart take flight.
In a world of jellyfish, so deep in the sea,
I lost myself in childhood dreams.

Goodbye Unspoken

I never said goodbye, you see,
A moment lost, a memory.
Papa, gone too soon, too fast,
A love that couldn't ever last.

His hands once steady, strong as stone,
Could fix the world, could build a home.
But not this time, not this fight,
His breath turned whispers, lost to night.

The air was thick, the house was still,
Grief a fog we couldn't kill.
Tears like rivers, voices hushed,
Even Daddy, the strong, my hero crushed.

I'd never seen him break before,
A giant humbled to the floor.
His sorrow cracked the world I knew,
If he could fall, then we could too.

And loss was cruel, it took its fill,
My dog lay quiet, the house grew still.
No wagging tail, no eager bark,
Just empty spaces, endless dark.

Then boxes stacked, a heavy load,
A new town, a different road.
But sorrow lingers, shadows stay,
No matter how far you move away.

I learned that year what endings mean,
That love can't always intervene.
That life moves on, the hurt remains,
A part of me still speaks their names.

A child's heart shouldn't carry this,
The weight of death, the loss, the miss.

Summer of '14

We came back home, back to the trees,
Where summer hummed in the Carolina breeze.
Sidewalks cracked but filled with life,
Barefoot races, laughter bright.
Neighbors weren't just faces near,
They were teammates, friends, the ones held dear.
We ruled the streets, the yards, the night,
Chasing goals in fading light.

World Cup fever in the air,
Flags we painted everywhere.
Brazil to Spain, red, white, and blue,
Every team, we cheered them on too.
Ball at feet, a dream so wide,
A thousand matches played outside.

Two small dogs yapped at our heels,
Boundless love, a joy so real.
We played as if we'd win it all.
Fireflies blinked, our crowd that roared.

We ran until our legs were sore.

No scoreboards, refs, or set-up plays,

Just golden, endless, perfect days.

Leaving Carolina Again

The road stretched long, the tires sighed,
As if they knew we'd left behind
More than just a house, a town,
But a life, roots deep in ground.

A backyard filled with barefoot days,
Laughter echoing in summer haze.
Neighbors who were more than friends,
A childhood built that met its end.

Papa's stone, a name carved deep,
The earth still holds the love we keep.
Beside him, beneath the pines,
Our old dog rests, no more signs.

Nana's voice, a warm embrace,
Fading now in time and space.
Aunts and cousins waving slow,
Knowing distance tends to grow.

The car moves on, the skyline fades,
Through windows streaked in sunlight shades.
California waits ahead,

But part of me stays here instead.

i am life—26

Golden State, Grey Mind

Sunset spills on foreign streets,
Mountains rise where oak trees leave.
New sky, new school, new quiet nights,
But nothing here feels quite right.

Laughter echoes from friends now ghosts,
Back home, back east, where love still grows.
I smile, I joke, I play along,
But the words feel hollow, the days feel wrong.

Fingertips tap, once, then twice,
Doorframes traced in silent rites.
A pattern whispered in my mind,
Touch this, then that—just one more time.

One more time and I'll feel fine,
One more time and I'll be safe.
One more time and all the weight
Of moving, missing, breaking, shifting
Might just pause—might stop existing.

I know it's strange, I know it's small,
But somehow it controls it all.
The thoughts scream loud but never speak,
Just loop and twist, deny relief.

I stare at hands, they look like mine,
But sometimes I don't feel real inside.
Like I'm just watching—just obeying—
Some unseen force that keeps replaying.

Don't let them see, don't let them know,
Brave face, straight spine, put on a show.

But in the dark, when no one sees,
I cry in silence, on hands and knees.

I tell myself, you'll be okay,
But echoes don't ever respond that way.

Through My Fingers

A ball at my feet, the sun in my eyes,
Running fast, kicking high,
Laughter rings, voices loud,
For a moment, I forget the clouds.

New hands to high-five, new names to learn,
Passes crisp, my feet take turns.
The weight still lingers, but fades with play,
Distractions turn to light each day.

Then the bell rings, halls stretch wide,
A sea of faces, side by side.
Middle school hums, a brand-new sound,
A trumpet's call, the drums resound.

Music swells, the notes take flight,
New friends form in brass and white.
Marching, playing, laughing, loud,

The past still knocks, the past still lingers,
But joy plays softly through my fingers.

Junior Ribs

The Outback buzzed, the menus spread,
With parents, cousin, drinks ahead.
The server came, her notepad tight,
Taking orders left and right.

Dad went first—Just water's fine.
Mom? Sweet tea, no lemon, light on ice.
My cousin called his usual pick,
And my brother's answer came out quick.

Then silence fell, it was my turn,
But all I'd thought—the ribs, they burned.
Not the drink, not what to say,
Just Junior ribs—locked in place.

For you? she asked, her gaze direct.
Junior ribs, I said—incorrect.
A pause so thick you'd need a knife,
A moment stretched, the worst of life.

The table stilled, I felt the weight,
A smirk from Dad—too late, too late.
The server blinked, then half a chuckle,
To drink? she asked, voice soft but subtle.

I scrambled fast— Oh, uh, soda.
A longer pause— felt imposing.
What kind? she asked, my throat went dry,
Cherry, I croaked, I wanted to die.

Cherry Coke or Cherry Sprite?
She tried again, polite, polite.
Yeah, I muttered, doomed to fate,
She nodded once, wrote down my take.

The drinks arrived, my ribs came too,
But shame still simmered, thick and true.
They laughed, of course, how could they not?
Junior ribs—I'd lost the plot.

To this day, when asked my sip,
I always think before I slip.

Unraveling

I run.
Feet pound dirt, breath pulls tight,
The world blurs past in streaks of light.
One step, one mile, one burning lung,
But I can't outrun what's in my mind.

I see them—
Laughing, easy, weightless, free,
Untouched by the knots inside of me.
They wake, they live, they simply be—
But I'm tangled in a war unseen.

Why me?
Why must my mind twist and fray,
Demanding rituals to keep fear away?
Why must I wake and fight to move,
While others just are—while they simply do?

I hide it well.
Jokes, routine, the push to stay strong,
But the anger grows, it drags along.

Resentment swells, sharp and mean,
At a world so bright when I'm unseen.

Yet I keep running.
One more day, one more try,
A step ahead, though lost inside.

Three Times, Three Times, Three Times

I let go.
Of the ball at my feet, the race on the track,
Of effort, of care, of looking back.
I let go, I let go, I let go—
Until nothing felt like mine to hold.

I was cruel.
Sharp words like knives, cutting deep,
Especially to her—the one who weeps.
She didn't deserve it, none of them did,
But I was a storm, and storms don't forgive.
I was cruel, I was cruel, I was cruel—
And I hated myself for it too.

I slipped.
From classes, from focus, from caring at all,
From running, from trying, I let myself fall.
I tried to scream, its voice in my brain,
Echoing fears that I couldn't explain.

I slipped, I slipped, I slipped—
And the world kept moving without me.

I shattered.
Panic rose like choking waves,
Death in the steam, thoughts wouldn't behave.
The shower, the silence, the weight of it all—
Too much, too much, I'd stumble, I'd fall.
I shattered, I shattered, I shattered—
And no one could hear the sound.

She was gone.
Small paws, quiet steps, a warmth now missing,
A sister left with no one to clean her eyes.
It was the second time I saw my dad cry.
I shattered, I shattered, I shattered—
Felt darkness's prying eye.

I burned.
Why was I the one who had to feel this?
Why did my mind twist and turn and choke?
Why did everyone else get to be normal?
I burned, I burned, I burned—
And the flames felt like the only thing that was mine.

I hated.
The way people smiled so easily,
The way they moved without hesitation.
The way they laughed—like nothing haunted them.
I hated, I hated, I hated—
Because it wasn't fair.

I told myself I didn't care,
That none of it mattered.
That if the world wouldn't make sense,
Then neither would I.

I was lost, a mind divorced.

It's Stupid

I started to speak,
Not to the world, but to her.
Her gentle voice, her calm eyes,
She listened, she understood,
And I felt safe for a while.

Momma sat close too,
Her heart laid bare,
Tears pooled,
A flood we both tried to contain.
I saw the weight I'd placed on her,
The scars left behind by my words,
My actions—
I never fully realized the toll.

I kept quiet at first,
Telling her what I thought was normal,
A stupid tick,
Something so small—so dumb.
But her words cut through the fog:

You know that sounds stupid, right?
No sugar coating, no easing in,
Just truth, clear and sharp.

I was taken aback,
Hurt, confused,
But there was something in that bluntness—
A shift I couldn't ignore.

It didn't fix me.
It didn't make the ticks disappear,
But it made me see them for what they were—

Unnecessary.

And for the first time,
I knew they didn't control me.

The advice wasn't kind,
But it was the best I'd ever get.

And I carry it with me,
Every single day—
The thought that still echoes in my mind:
It's stupid.

I let it stick.
And little by little,
I learned to let go and fight back.

But goddamn, OCD is a bitch.

-Interlude-

Mental illness is a battle. Some days, it's just background noise. Other days, it's a full-on boss fight with no health potions left. And if you've ever felt like you're fighting it alone, I need you to know—you're not.

OCD is annoying. It's like having an overbearing backseat driver in your own brain, constantly telling you that if you don't do something just right, the world might explode. My OCD is manageable now, but that didn't happen overnight. It took years of learning to roll my eyes at the intrusive thoughts instead of obeying them.

Now, for anyone out there struggling—OCD, depression, anxiety, anything—you are not alone. I don't care if it feels like no one understands or if you think nobody would notice if you were gone. Because someone does. Someone would. And if you truly believe no one in your life cares, then let me be the first to say: I care. So that's at least one.

Robin Williams once said, *Suicide is a permanent solution to a temporary problem.* And he was right. If I had given up when I was 13, I would have missed out on so much. The best friendships of my life. Some of the funniest, sweetest moments. I would have never known how good life could get. In fact, my story would have ended here. Look at how much of the book is left! And you—yeah, you—there's more waiting for you too. You might not see it yet, but trust me, it's there.

So if you're struggling, reach out. Talk to someone. A friend, a family member, a teacher, a therapist, a random stranger who gives off good vibes—whoever. If you're in the U.S., you can call or text 988 for the Suicide & Crisis Lifeline.
For international support, visit findahelpline.com.

Take your meds if you need them. Go to therapy if you can. Do whatever helps. Fight. Then fight again. And then fight some more.

Because you deserve to be here. And I hope you stick around to see what happens next.

Alright—deep breath. That was heavy, but it needed to be said. Now, let's get back to it. There are a ton of good poems up ahead, so buckle in. We've got a journey to continue.

–Interlude Over–

A New Fixation

The world shut down,
And so did I.
The days blurred,
In and out of the same four walls.
I fought back,
Little by little—
Against the chaos in my mind,
The OCD, the anger, the hurt.
And I tried,
I tried so hard,
To be better.
To be better for her—
For my mother.

Then my friend said it,
Her voice cut through the screen,
I watch anime.
I laughed,
Mocked her at first,
Because it seemed so silly,

So strange—
How could that be anything worth watching?

But she was patient,
She didn't let me go.
She convinced me,
To watch just a little more.

I fell asleep at first,
Half-hearted, uninterested.
But then something shifted—
After a few episodes,
I was hooked.

It was the story,
It was the animation,
It was the world,
A world I could lose myself in.

I dove deeper.
I devoured every episode,
Every book.
The manga,
The characters,

The stories—they became me.
The more I read,
The more I needed to know,
I collected,
This new passion,

A new fixation.

Locked up at home,
With nothing else but time,
It became my escape.
It became my world.
I found something to hold onto,
To care about—

And though the world outside was quiet,
Inside, I was screaming—
But at least now,
I had something to scream for.

Shifting Light

Anime filled the gaps,
Every frame a new world to escape,
Every page a story I could hold close.
The obsession grew,
But so did I—
Each book, each episode,
A step towards something better.

OCD loosened its grip,
Little by little,
Fighting back,
Like a storm that slowly calms.
It didn't vanish,
But I learned how to breathe again.

Weekends meant shopping trips,
The collection growing,
The shelves filling,
As if each new addition

Was another victory
In a long fight.

I found a job,
A soccer referee—
The itch never left me,
The game still called.
I raised the flag,
Ran the field,
And felt a piece of me return.

I stopped crying the way I used to.
Grief softened, like waves retreating,
leaving only footprints of what once was.

They left, one by one,
a slow unraveling—
Grandma's warm hands,
Grandpa's deep voice,
a wagging tail that never stilled,
an uncle's laughter echoing in rooms now quiet.

But death did not take them.
Not really.

I carry them in the way I tie my shoes,
in the recipes I never quite get right,
in the stories I tell without meaning to.
They are not gone—
only woven into the fabric of me.

And so I do not cry like I should.
Maybe I do not grieve the way they expect.
But I live,
and they live through me.

I was starting to shed
The weight of anger,
The hurt I'd kept inside,
Leaking out like darkness fading—
The rudeness,
The words I couldn't take back,
Slowly disappeared.

Me and my brother—
Closer than ever,
No more petty fights,
Just shared moments,
Laughter, understanding.

A bond that grew stronger
With every day that passed.

And I,
Was becoming happier—
No longer lost in the shadows.

With every step,

The light crept closer,

And the darkness,

It stayed behind.

Unforgettable Moment

The weekend came, excitement grew,
A world of dreams in front of view.
I met the voice, the one I knew,
A moment I'd never outgrew.

Nervous, but my heart was true,
A dream I thought I'd never pursue.
We spoke, and in that time I knew,
This memory would forever renew.

Anime Gods and Novices

Back in middle school,
I saw him with blue hair,
A flash of color,
A style beyond compare.

Fast forward to sophomore year,
The mask we both wore.

PE together, hours of chat,
Filling the time with all that we had.
He, the anime god,
I, a novice in the crowd,
Yet together we skipped class,
Immersed in worlds unbowed.

Our bond grew stronger,
As friendships do,
Anime shared,
Old and new.

A beautiful friendship,
Built on time well spent,
Through masked faces
And hours well lent.

Our Great Escape

We hatched a plan,
To skip school that day,
Climbing the fence,
And running away.

I threw my backpack,
Climbed over first,
Turning to see him,
A scene quite reversed.

Stuck by his shirt,
Arms flailing in the air,
Searching for freedom,
But going nowhere.

"Got scissors?" he pleaded,
I stared and replied,
What? Sorry, no—
Those aren't in my supplies..

People walked by,
But I couldn't just stare,
While my anime god
Was stuck in despair.

Finally, with a rip,
He broke free from the bind,
Coming down hard,
With no grace in mind.

He hid behind trash cans,
Changed into PE shorts,
We laughed, we high-fived,
Our great escape had worked.

Convention

My first con with my anime god,
Merch bags heavy, wallet gone.
Met new voices, shook their hands,
Autographs, prints—dreams unplanned.
Crowds were wild, the hype was loud,
I left that place, an anime god.

That Night at the Italian Restaurant

A new job, excitement in the air,
But the night took a turn I didn't prepare.
A cut, a slip—
Then nothing but the dark—
Two times I passed out,
A silent, spinning arc.

It was the one night,
I didn't wear my glasses—

A firefighter came,
Mustache thick and neat,
Had me doing high knees,
Trying to find my feet.

He's always this white?
He asked my dad with a grin.
Dad just nodded,
Said, Yeah, that's him.

The night blurred together—
A memory, sharp and stark,
Of a moment that burned,
Leaving quite a funny mark.

Winds

We laughed, we ran, we made our plans,
But winds can shift like shifting sands.
One voice whispered, pulled me wide,
I followed blind, left friends behind.

No anger burned, no hate took hold,
Just distance carved in silence cold.
Paths diverged, as seasons do,
But I still smile when I think of you.

Roads Anew

Freedom sat in the form of keys,
Heavy metal, light as a breeze.
No more waiting, no more rides,
Just open roads and midnight skies.

I gripped the wheel, heart held tight,
Manhood whispered in the night.
Not just driving, but standing tall,
Learning respect, learning to call.

No more sharp words, no bitter tones,
No cutting down, no sticks, no stones.
I saw the weight my words once threw,
And vowed to shape a kinder view.

Each stoplight blinked, a lesson learned,
Each turn I took, a page I turned.
Not just roads, but paths anew,
Becoming better, pushing through.

Reaching Back

The space between us was measured in silence,

a road once walked now overgrown.

Not by hate, not by fire,

just by time left alone.

I had listened to the wrong voice,
let a friend turn me away.
Told myself it was fine,
that maybe he'd be okay.

But guilt lingers like dust in the air,
never heavy enough to break you,
but always there.

He told me to stop being friends with my anime god,
said he had problems,

said he wasn't right,
but I knew it wasn't true,
knew he just needed a better guide,
knew he just needed a friend.
Still, I left without a fight.
And what did I get in return?

A slow unraveling,
a drifting away,
until that same friend
who turned me from others
turned from me one day.
No reason, no fight,
just a casual goodbye,
like I was an old book
they had no reason to try.

I wasn't struggling,
wasn't in pain,
but I wasn't happy either,
just existing,
just staying the same.

Then one day,
I reached out first—
a message, a step,
a hand through the past.
I told my anime god I wanted to talk,
that I'd made mistakes,
that I'd walked the wrong path.

We met in person,
face to face,
no fire, no cold,
just two people,
still standing, still whole.

We spoke, and the cracks filled in,
like rain finding the spaces between stone.
Not perfect, not polished,
but something real, something known.

And then, like fate stitching things whole,
another voice called my name,
I turned to see an old friend,
one I thought had done the same.

i am life—62

Can I get a ride to work?
No resentment, no weight,
just a question from them, just a step,
just a chance to set things straight.

As we walked, silence sat heavy,
but I cracked it open with words.
Spilled out all my mistakes,
let the truth finally be heard.
And they listened—no anger, no doubt,
just nodded, just took it.
They said, we miss you, it was straight and flatout.

The next day, I walked back to the group,
unsure what I would find.
But they were there, with open arms,
no hate, no judgment, just love realigned.

Some friendships fade, some come undone,
but some, if given a chance,
find their way back to where they belong.

Takeout Cheap

Culinary class—should've chilled,
but leave it to me to nearly set ablaze
the whole school, chocolate killed.

A little heat, maybe too much,
—oh, look, flames greet!

Panic set in, alarms screamed loud,
my classmates scattered, a frantic crowd.

The teacher rushed, extinguisher in hand,
Andy, what the hell—this wasn't the plan!
Smoke curled, my shame ran deep,
Guess I won't be cooking—better stick to takeout
cheap.

Doors Are Wide

Love felt easy, light as air,
like it was always, meant to be there.

Then came a trip, a dream, a ride,
Disneyland nights with friends by my side.
We ran through streets of neon glow,
laughing, shouting, taking it slow.

The friend who once had called my name,
slept beside me, like old times came.
No grudges held, no wounds remained,
just tired smiles, friendships sustained.

The fireworks burst, the castle gleamed,
a childhood wish, a place once dreamed.
We rode till late, we sang out loud,
in the happiest place, lost in the crowd.

Then back to school, a final stretch,
senior year now at its edge.

One last bell, one last class,
one last time we'd walk those paths.

Then gowns were donned, the moment near,
nerves and pride, a mix sincere.
I saw my anime god stand tall,
we made it through—we conquered all.

My family came from far away,
to see me walk, to hear them say,
my name out loud, my steps so sure,
the future wide, the past secure.

Hugs so tight, no words could speak,
just love that day, so strong, unique.
A chapter closed, a door swung wide,
the next unknown—but my arms spread wide.

Bittersweet

The house emptied box by box,
the walls echoed a little louder each day.
I watched my parents pack up their lives,
watched my childhood tuck itself away.

They were moving forward,
and I had a choice—
follow the path I'd always known,
or stand on my own with my own voice.

I'd built something here,
a life worth holding tight.
Friends, love, a future unfolding,
something told me this was right.

Saying goodbye felt sharp and strange,
not like the moves we'd made before.
This time, it wasn't just them leaving—
this time, I stayed behind the door.

I was chasing manhood,
stepping forward alone.
It was bittersweet, but it was mine—
a path I'd finally grown.

Love Written at Dawn

Love felt easy, then it was gone,
a fleeting warmth before the dawn.

It hurt, of course, but I let it flow,
let sorrow breathe, then let it go.
No desperate reach, no bitter bite,
just quiet nights and morning light.

My friends stood tall, some steady guys,
anchors beneath unsteady skies.
They held me firm when I'd collapse,
reminding me of all that lasts.

I saw my faults, laid bare, unshrouded,
the weight of care, too heavy, clouded.

I'd traced her kindness, ignored the cracks,
chased a dream that gave none back.

But love is not a hollow prize,
nor built on hope with shuttered eyes.
So I vowed to stand, to see, to know,

to walk ahead, not just let go.
Not bitter, not broken, not lost in despair,
but moving forward— I'd be aware.

Love Written at Dusk

I was not lost when I met you.
I was steady, sure, whole.
But then you walked in—
not as some guiding light,
but as something sharper, louder, more.
I was already standing in the sun,
and yet somehow, you still burned brighter.

Your ethereal eyes—
Not just dreamily dark, or devastatingly deep—
they were the color of promises whispering me to
sleep,
words I should have never believed.
They were earth cracked and waiting for rain,
a wildfire disguised as warmth,
the last flicker of light before a star dies.
And still, I let them pull me in.

You did me wrong.
I know that.

And I could sit here and act like I don't care,
but the way it ended—
that's what cut the deepest.
The leaving wasn't wrong,
but how it was done was.
I always like to end things right.
Even when it hurts, even when it's over,
I need to walk away knowing I gave it everything,
knowing I was honest, knowing we were real.
But you,
You let it fall apart like it was nothing.
Like it never meant anything.
No closure, no honesty, just silence where words—
You let it rot instead of laying it to rest.

And while I'm being honest, I know,
I wasn't good enough either.
Not in the way you needed me to be.
I wasn't careless or cruel,
but I wasn't what you wanted.
I cared too much, in all the wrong ways,
held on too tightly when I should've loosened my grip,
spoke when I should've listened,

stayed silent when you needed words.
I thought maybe loving you was enough,
but love without understanding is just noise,
just hands reaching but never quite holding.

We weren't horrible,
but we weren't great.
And maybe that's the part that stings the most.

Somehow, there's still a part of me that would do it
all over again,
I would take it all,
even knowing how the story ends.

You know I'm a sucker for love.
When they ask if I'd go if you beckoned,
I don't say no right away.
Even now, my heart hesitates,
knowing full well it's not right,
but not wanting to stop.

I should be smarter.
I am smarter.
I should keep walking, let time do its work,

but my hands still remember the way you fit against me,

and my heart,

it still skips at the thought of you.

I would walk through the embers again, barefoot, unflinching,

just for one more moment,

one more second with you.

I know I shouldn't.

I know I can't.

But sometimes, I don't want to be smart.

Sometimes, I don't want to be strong.

Sometimes, I want to be that same boy,

blinded by love, reckless in devotion,

willing to set himself on fire just to keep you warm.

So, no matter how much I heal,

somehow, I still miss the fire.

If you reached for me, I might forget why we shouldn't be—my mind twirling.

At least meet me in Montauk, pretty girl.

Onward

I moved forward, somewhat steady and sure,
no weight too heavy, no wound too pure.
The past had shaped me, but it didn't define.
I walked with purpose, this path was mine.

Conventions called, lights and crowds,
laughing with my anime god, voices loud.
A new friend, the one with the red stripe,
fitting in like stars in the night.

Summer stretched, golden and free,
nights of stories, days of peace.

Then college came, a world unknown,
but I found my place, made it my own.

A professor wise, a mentor strong,
lessons deeper, minds drawn along.

Though my friends were spread apart,
we fought for time, we held our hearts.

Dinners shared, movies played,
memories made that never fade.
Life had tried to pull us wide,
but we stood firm, side by side.

And through it all, thick and thin,
I knew I'd fight, I'd rise, I'd win.

Time

North Carolina, a house so wide,
a theater inside, with seats that recline.

With my brother, we laughed and roamed,
a place so big, yet still felt home.

Then Christmas came, I flew alone,
sky stretched wide, yet I had grown.

My parents waited, arms held tight,
the home was bright with winter light.
Stories shared, the year gone by,
love unshaken, time can't pry.

SacAnime 25'

Three days lost in neon lights,
figures, posters, endless sights.
Wallet wept, but joy ran high,
laughter echoed, time flew by.

Red streaks bright, a glass held tall,
Anime God led the toast for all.
A weekend carved in memory's glow,
one of the best—I'd always know.

A Writer too????

I spent my days in stories deep,
in books and shows, in dreams and sleep.
I loved the worlds that others made,
but something in me wouldn't fade.

An ember burned, a quiet spark,
a tale I'd held within my heart.
Since junior year, it called my name,
but life had kept me in its frame.

Yet nights grew long, and time felt tight,
consuming worlds lost all its light.
Not that I had lost the love,
but something new was rising up.

No longer just a watcher's view,
I'd build a world, I'd see it through.
Through sleepless nights, my hands took flight—
See You Later, Brother came to life.

i am life-79

i am life

I have learned to forgive, to let things be,
To unearth the quiet roots that set me free.
I've learned to move forward, to loosen my grasp,
To surrender control, to take off the mask.
A part of me is who I'm not,
A lesson earned, a truth well-fought.

The ones beside me lift me high,
Like winds beneath the wings that try.
They let me bask—no judgment, no wall,
In laughter, in love, in moments so small.
For in the smallest moments, I find my peace,
A quiet that softens, where sorrows cease.

No hate in my heart, no enemy exists,
Just souls like mine, all facing their fears.
I dream of accepting the apologies unmet, a longing,
but closure, I don't need to get.

For if I carry the same old bricks,
I'll build the same old house, the same old tricks.

i am life—80

So why choose a familiar hell,
When the unknown heaven could serve so well?

The seats are empty, the stage is bare,
Yet why do ghosts still linger there?
If you are love, then let it show—
A fire withheld will never glow.
Grief is love with nowhere to go,
A river still flowing beneath the snow.

I do not cry the way I should,
But I carry their names, their lessons, their good.
You're allowed to miss someone each day,
And still be glad they walked away.

I mostly miss the dream of us,
The hope of what we'd grow into.
But summer comes, the heat still burns,
And most every wave brings thoughts of—

My comfort zone is where dreams fade,
So I step through fear, unafraid.
I chase my passions with utter ferocity,
For late brilliance is worse than on-time mediocrity.

We judge others by what they do,
Yet measure ourselves by thoughts untrue.
Take a breath, reflect, and see—
Is the person you are who you've chosen to be?
I sought freedom in distant lands,
In hands that swore they'd understand.

But home is not in another's bones,
It's carried within, in seeds I've sown.
Being good means being free,
That's what I believe.
If I am good at what I do,
If I am kind and strong and true,
Then I am free.

Freedom's not a thing to find,
But something to breathe, something to be.
The hands that build, the chains I break,
The moments of love, the mistakes I make.
A true warrior knows not to fight,
But when to walk away from spite.

Strength is not in blows returned,
But in lessons lived, in wisdom earned.

i am life—82

I climb each peak with tireless stride,
Yet my mind denies the mountain's crest,
Refusing my ambition, its moments rest.

After my parents left, I knew I'd be fine,
Not broken—just shifted in the hands of time.

The poorest soul I've ever seen
Had wealth, but neither soul nor dream.

Why take life so seriously?
One day, we'll all be pushing up daisies.

I will express, for I am human,
For crying is joy—don't confuse them.
I am wisdom found after the rain,
Proof that loss does not end in pain.
I am him, I am her, I am all I ever knew.
I am the past, the sky, hell even the sea—
And life itself lives inside of me.

Being a Branham means I can do anything,
That's what my father told me, and I'm believing.
Branham is not just a name, but a solid creed,
A lineage of strength, of will, of deed.

i am life—83

I am the song in a silent room,
The flowers that bloom atop their tomb.

Through every storm, I'll find my stride,
No matter the weight, no matter the tide.
The past may haunt, the future unknown,
But I'll face it all, even if I'm alone.

No fall too deep, no road too long,
I'll rise again, keep moving strong.
Through hurt and loss, through joy and fear,
Each step brings me closer, the path is clear.

I walk toward a new day, yonder,
Where dreams are born, and hearts grow fonder.
Whatever life throws, I'll face it still,
Pushing forward, I always will.

I am the scars, the fight, the light,
The stars that pierce the night.
Rights and wrongs, hues and blues,
I am everything you see.
Light from dark, I will rise anew,
i am life. And so are you.

Afterword

Writing this book has been an experience unlike any other. I poured my heart into these pages, revisiting the past and looking toward the future. Every struggle, every triumph, every little moment—they all led me here. I knew I'd have to leave out lots of important moments in my life to keep things at the pace I wanted. These are just the moments that have stuck with me most after nineteen years. Sorry if I left anything big out!

Something I've been asked a lot is how I write so much. People tell me they could never write a book, and I never have a great—or even good—answer for them. I usually just say, "haha yeah idk," and move on. But writing this afterword has made me really think, not just about how I write so much, but why I write in the first place.

To answer the first question... haha yeah, I still don't know. Sorry, but I don't have some profound answer for that one. I've never truly hit writer's block the way people expect. I hit brick walls, sure, but I just climb over them. That's the whole point of a wall—to figure out how to get past it. (For how to climb the wall, see the poem, "Our Great Escape.") In all seriousness, I write and write and write. That's how I produce so much. I keep going, even when it's tough.

But, why, that one, I do have an answer for. I write because I'm passionate about art, about storytelling, and about putting something positive into the world. If anything I write ever impacts just one person in a meaningful way, then I've achieved all I could ever want. That's the whole reason I do this.

Creating *Love Written at Dawn* and *Love Written at Dusk* was an experience in itself. They ended up being some of my favorites in this collection. *Dawn* is how I like to think I handle things. It's mature, self-aware, accepting. But in the recesses of my mind, *Dusk* is there. Because with maturity comes immaturity. No matter how much we grow, there's always that small part of us that still feels, still wants, still burns, even when we know better.

Also, I definitely listened to way too much of *Cigarettes After Sex* at two in the morning, so *Dusk* is what came out of that.

I'm already in the works on my next book—which is actually a series—called *Wishes in Another World*. I've been juggling both *i am life* and *Wishes in Another World*, and it's been great. I'm about a fifth of the way through its story, and it's been such a fun journey. If I had to sum it up in just a few words, I'd say it's about personal growth. I can't wait for people to read it!

I want to take a second to say thank you. To my family, my friends, and anyone who's been a part of this journey, whether you realize it or not. To the people who have challenged me, pushed me, supported me, and even those who made things difficult—because in the end, you all shaped me in one way or another.

Maybe in a few years, I'll look back and be repulsed at some parts of this book, laugh at others, and realize how much more I still have to figure out. But if there's one thing I've learned, it's that every story is ongoing. Life doesn't wrap up neatly like a book does. It keeps going, twisting in ways you never expect.

So, for now, this is where I leave things. Hopefully, nothing too crazy happens—or I'll have to start writing *i am life 2: Electric Boogaloo.*

Until then—I'll see you later. Keep moving forward.

—Andy Branham

Roll the credits...

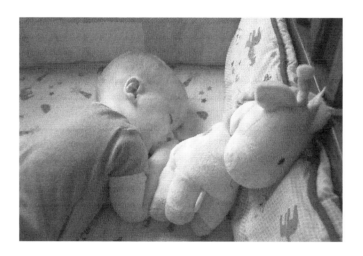

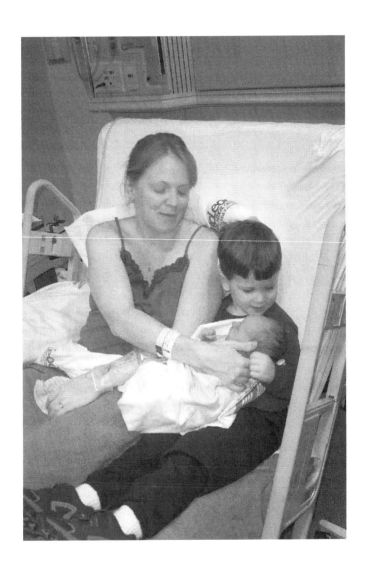

i am life-92

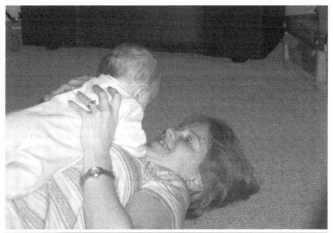

i am life—93

Merry Christmas

The Branhan

i am life-94

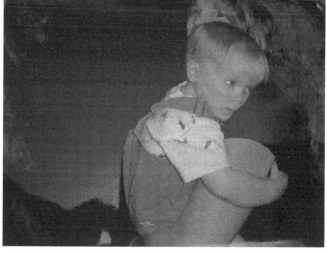

i am life-95

i am life- 96

i am life-97

i am life-98

i am life—99

i am life-100

i am life—102

i am life—103

i am life—105

i am life—106

i am life—107

i am life-108

i am life—110

i am life-111

i am life-112

i am life–113

i am life-114

i am life—115

i am life–116

i am life—117

i am life—118

i am life-1??

i am life—123

i am life-124

i am life—125

i am life—126

i am life—127

i am life—128

i am life—129

i am life—130

i am life—13?

i am life-133

i am life—134

i am life–135

i am life-136

i am life-137

i am life—138

One day,

I'll reach 140...

Made in the USA
Las Vegas, NV
07 April 2025

7cf78fdf-0345-4ac2-acc0-9582745f6c08R01